J 1767697

MAPS AND MAP-MAKING

Mark C.W. Sleep

Wayland

YOUNG EXPLORER

Maps and Map-making
Rivers and Streams
Hills and Mountains
Roads, Railways and Canals
Around the Coast
Where Plants Grow
Where People Live
Farms and Farming

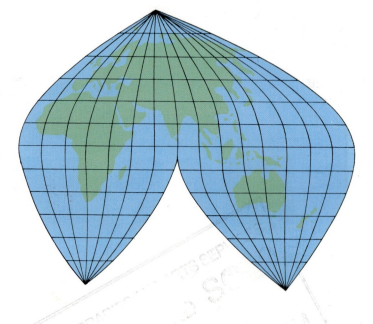

Acknowledgements
The photographs used in this book were supplied by the following: Bruce Coleman: (Eric Crichton) 17 (top left), (Fritz Prenzel) 17 (top right).

The Ordnance Survey maps are extracts from the following: the 1975 1:10 000 map 14 (left), the 1980 1:1250 map 14 (right), the 1980 1:50 000 map 17 (left), the 1974 1:50 000 map 17 (right), the 1981 1:50 000 map 31. All are reproduced with the permission of the Controller of Her Majesty's Stationery Office (Crown Copyright reserved).

The remaining maps are reproduced with the permission of the following: the Australian Division of National Mapping (Crown Copyright reserved) 29; the Buckley Map Studio 15; The New Zealand Department of Land and Survey (Crown Copyright reserved) 17; the U.S. Geological Survey 16.

First published in 1983 by Wayland Publishers Limited
49 Lansdowne Place, Hove, East Sussex BN3 1HF, England
© Copyright 1983 Wayland Publishers Limited

ISBN 0 85078 273 2

Illustrated and designed by John Yates
Typeset by The Grange Press, Butts Road, Southwick, Sussex
Printed in Italy by G Canale & C.S.p.A., Turin

Contents

1. Looking at maps
What is a map?   4
Scale   5

2. Making maps
A family map   6
Mapping your home   7
Compass bearings   8
Taking a bearing   9
Mapping your local park   10
Drawing your map   11
Keys and symbols   12

3. Survey maps
Fixing a survey   13
Large- and small-scale maps   14
Contour lines   16
Grid references   18
Six-figure grid references   19

4. Atlasses
The round earth   20
Covering the globe with a map   21
Shapes and areas   22
Latitude and longitude   24
The 'norths'   26

5. Using maps
Maps on walks   27
Maps on cycle rides   28
Maps on car journeys   30

Glossary   32

Index   32

1. Looking at maps

What is a map?

With an adult, visit the top of the highest tower or tallest building in your town. Try to look straight down out of a window. Be careful, though, and do not lean out too far.

What do you notice about the size of the cars, the people, the roads and the pavements?

Take a photograph or make an accurate drawing of all that you see below you.

Have you ever been up in an aeroplane? At much greater heights, what sort of view do you get?

A map is like a bird's-eye view of somewhere. Maps are used to show the various positions of different things, such as countries, or roads, railways, and rivers. A map can be drawn for almost everything – the distribution of birds, or butterflies, rocks, trees and soils.

Visit a map shop and look at the different sorts of maps that you can buy.

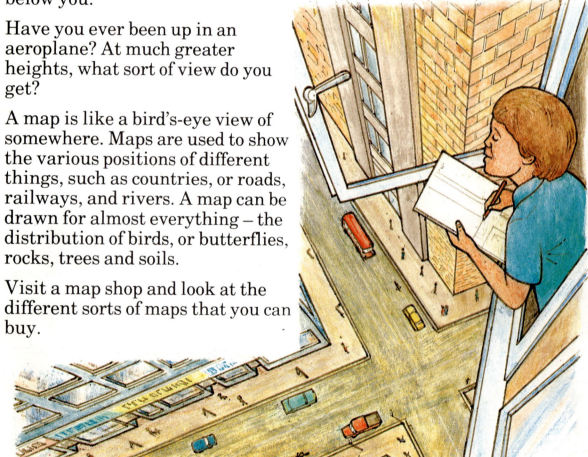

Scale

Examine more closely the drawing or photograph you made of the view from your tower or tall building. Although it is much smaller than real life, it looks right because everything has been reduced in size by the same amount. It has been reduced to scale.

Work out the scale of your drawing or photograph by measuring the width of your tall building in your picture and in real life. If the base of the building is 10 m wide on the ground, but is 10 cm wide on your picture, then your scale is:
10 cm to 10 m
or 1 cm to 1 m
or 1 cm to 100 cm
or 1:100

On real maps, the scale can be shown in different ways. Sometimes it is written in figures: 1:1 250 or 1:50 000. Sometimes it is written as 1 cm to 1 km or 1 in to 1 mile, and sometimes it is shown as a bar divided into km or miles like those below.

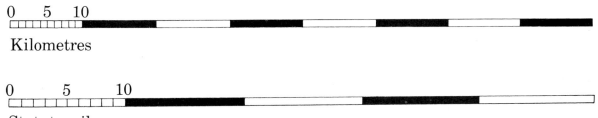

2. Making maps

A family map

Trace an outline map of your country from an atlas. Mark where you were born and any other places where you have lived before your present home. Mark each place with the dates during which you lived there. Join them up in correct order. Add arrows and your initials to the line.

Now add lines for your parents, grandparents and as many generations as you can.

Use different colours for each generation.

Some families will need to use a world outline map instead of one for a single country, state or county.

Compare your family map with those of some of your friends.

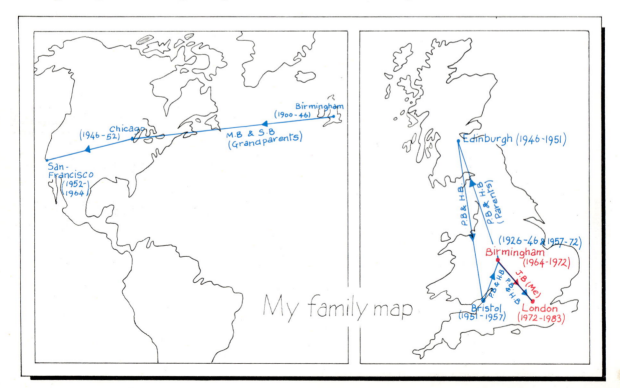

Mapping your home

You can draw an accurate map of your home, garden or favourite room in your house.

First make a sketch diagram in a notebook. Then measure in paces, or with a tape measure, the length and width of the area and other important distances such as the widths of doors and gates. Record all the measurements on your sketch drawing.

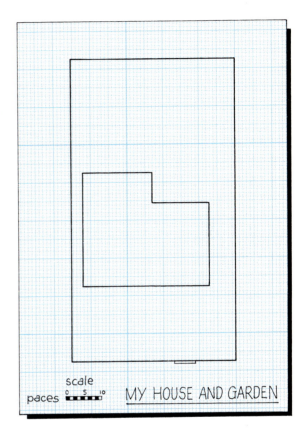

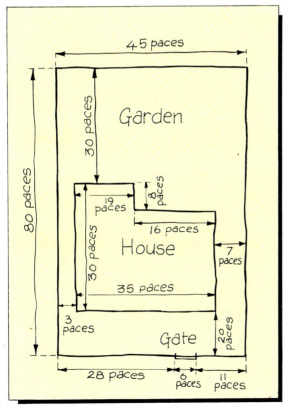

Sketch map

Now take a piece of squared graph paper and choose a suitable scale such as 1 cm to 1 pace or 1 m (½ in to 3 ft). Check that your paper is wide enough to include the whole of your map at this scale.

Draw your map to scale on the graph paper. Add a title and show the scale you have used.

Compass bearings

The circumference of any circle, such as that around the face of a compass, can be divided into 360 parts. Each of these parts is called one degree (1°). The bearing of any object or feature is the distance, in degrees, measured in a clockwise direction from north.

The best type of compass to use when taking bearings is the Silva-type compass. But you can make a similar compass yourself.

The circle below has been divided into seventy-two sections, each of 5°. Trace this circle on to a piece of tracing paper and then glue this paper on a large piece of thick card. Now extend each line outwards as far as possible. Mark each line in degrees, at 5° intervals, starting from 0°. You have made a 'bearing board'.

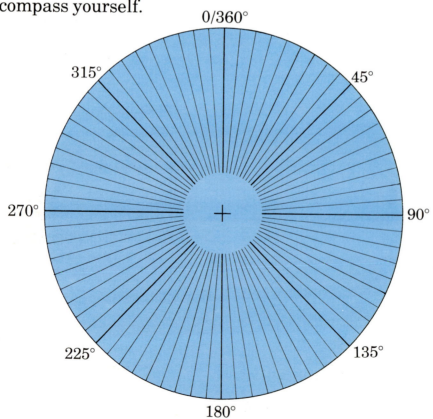

Taking a bearing

To take a bearing, lay your bearing board on a box on the ground. Place a pocket compass in the centre of the board with the north sign pointing towards 0°/360°. Now rotate the board until the needle of the compass is pointing towards north. Remove the compass, without moving the board.

Now place a ruler on its edge on to the board so that one edge crosses the centre. By looking along the top edge of the ruler, you can take bearings of all the different objects in, say, your town square.

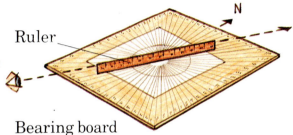

In the picture below, the hotel will have a bearing of 40°, the church 85°, the baker's shop 260°, and the telephone box 330°.

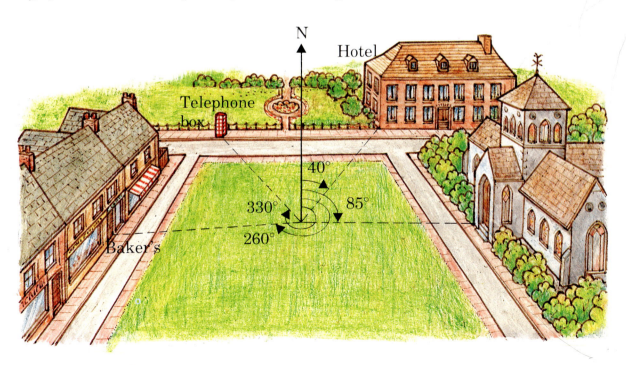

Mapping your local park

You can draw a very accurate map of your local park using your compass and bearing board.

Draw a large sketch map as you did for the map of your house or garden (see page 7). Mark in all the important paths, roadways, landmarks and buildings that you want to include on your final map.

Now find a suitable position from which you can see most of the features in your park. This 'base point' should be fairly central but it should not be near ironwork since this will affect the compass.

From this base point take bearings of all the important features of the park using your compass and bearing board.

Record the bearings and pace the distances between the base point and each feature.

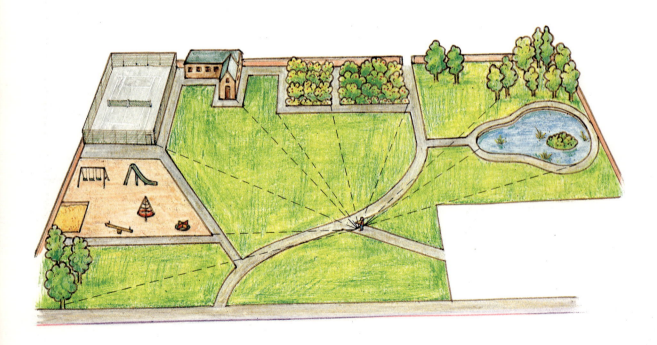

Drawing your map

Draw your map on a piece of squared graph paper.
Choose a suitable scale in the same way as you did for your home map.
In the centre of the paper, mark and label your original base point.
Now trace the circle from page 8 again and use this to mark the bearings on to your map. With north at the top of the graph paper, mark in the directions of all the bearings faintly in pencil. Mark off the distances to scale that you measured in the park.

You can now draw in all the important features of your map and rub out all the rough pencil lines.

Add a title, a scale and a north sign.

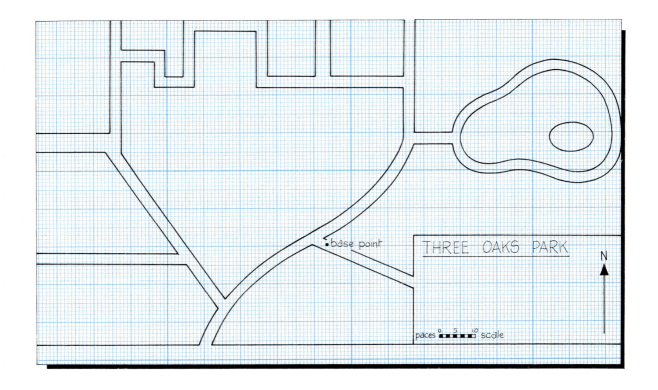

Keys and symbols

Add labelling, shading and symbols to your map to explain the different features. For example, grassland can be shaded green and water blue.

The map below will give you an idea of the kind of symbols to use for other features, but you can always make up your own. Now add a key to your map to show the meaning of the symbols and shading.

Your accurate drawing is now complete with title, scale, key and north sign.

Try making other maps of your street or school playing field.

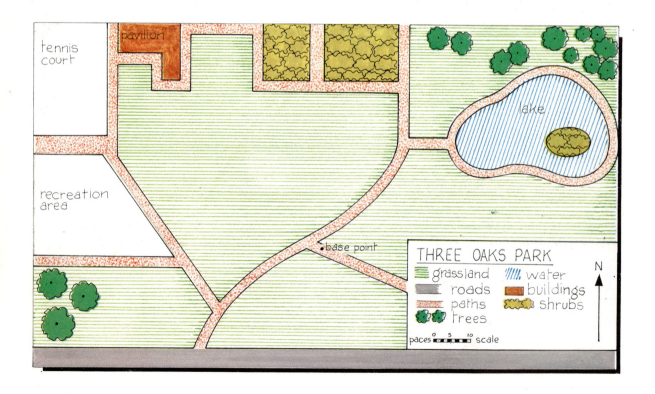

3. Survey maps

Fixing a survey

Most countries of the world have their own regional survey maps with different shadings and symbols showing different features. In the same way that you started your park map from a fixed base point (see page 10) so a country has to fix an origin for its maps.

In Britain, the origin is fixed at a point to the south and west of the furthest point of land. From here, a grid of 100-km squares has been drawn up across the whole of the country. Each 100-km square is given a two-letter code. The 100-km squares are further sub-divided into the 1-km squares which appear on most modern maps produced by the Ordnance Survey.

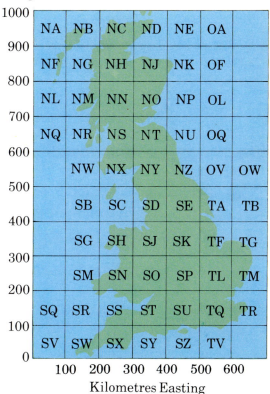

Australia, Canada and the U.S.A. are so large that no single point of origin is used. Each state produces its own survey which is then made up into an atlas of the whole country. There is no standard grid system in these countries either, although many states now use the 100-km and 1-km grid system.

Large- and small-scale maps

A large-scale map is one on which a large area of map covers quite a small area of country. A small-scale map is one on which a small area of map covers quite a large area of country.

The best scale of map for general purposes is the 1:50 000 or the 1 in to 1 mile (1:63 360) map. For walking, the 1:25 000 or the 2½ in to 1 mile scale is best.

Local service companies, like gas and electricity, use the 1:10 000 scale map. On these, individual buildings can be seen. Builders, surveyors and planners use even larger-scale maps – 1:2 500 or even 1:1 250.

The two maps below are of an area of London on 1:10 000 and 1:1 250 scale maps.

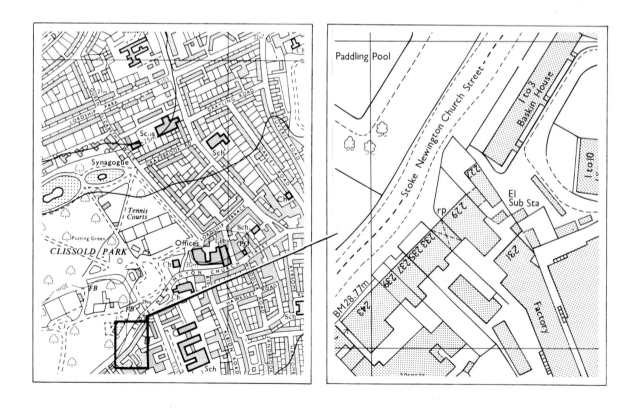

Smaller-scale maps of 1:100 000 are better as regional or area maps, whilst maps with scales of 1:1 000 000 or 1:2 500 000 cover large areas of a country in one sheet and are excellent as route-planning maps. The 1-km squares are usually left off these maps.

The map below is a 1:2 500 000-scale map of the Cape Town area of South Africa. Compare it with a map of your country drawn to a similar scale.

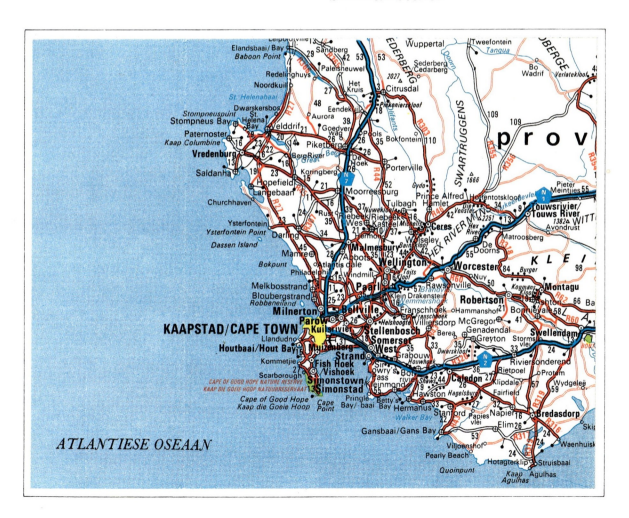

Contour lines

Contour lines are the lines drawn on large-scale maps to show hills and valleys. They join points of equal height above sea level. Some lines are marked with their height in metres or feet.

Look at the contour lines on a large-scale map of your area. Try to identify the hills and valleys shown on the map.

Closely-packed contour lines mean that the slopes are steep. If the contour lines are widely spaced it means that the slopes are more gentle. If there are hardly any contour lines, the area is probably almost flat.

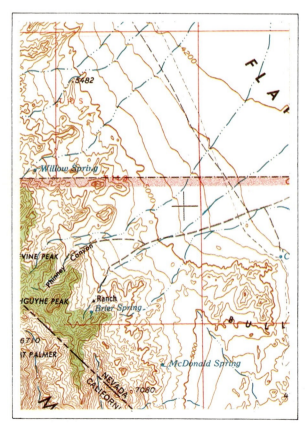

How contour lines are drawn

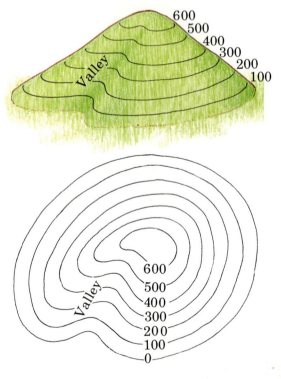

Look at the following map extracts and the photographs of the features they are showing.

If contour lines end very abruptly at a coastline then it means that there is a sheer drop to the sea, in other words, there are cliffs.

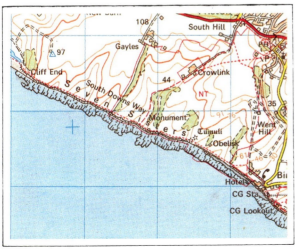

A volcano will look like this:

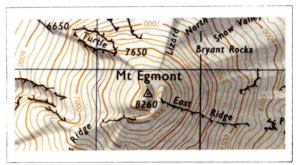

A valley will look like this:

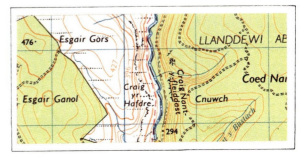

17

Grid references

Grid references are used to pin-point the exact position of something on a large-scale map. The 100-km squares can be divided into smaller 1-km squares (see page 13). So, inside each 100-km square, a grid is produced of one hundred lines running north to south, called eastings. These measure the distance east from the origin. The one hundred lines running east to west are called northings. Northings measure the distance north from the origin.

Each 1-km square is identified by the letter code for its 100-km square, followed by four figures. The eastings are always read before the northings.

If you were standing in the shaded 1-km square, within the large 100-km square, SO, you would be standing in the square SO2010.

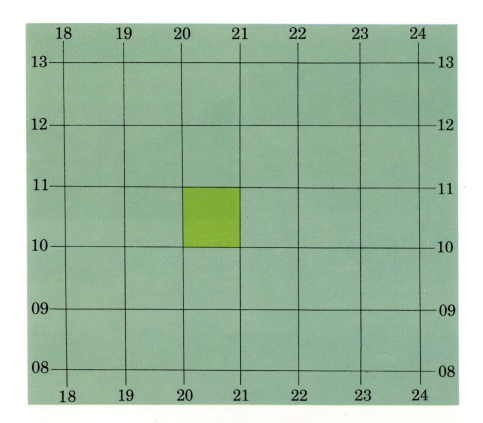

18

Six-figure grid references

In order to pin-point a position more accurately within a 1-km square, a six-figure grid reference can be produced by estimating the distance of the position east of the easting and north of the northing.

So the church in square SO2010 is given the six-figure reference SO 208 105. The 8 is added after 20 because the church is approximately eight-tenths of the distance between easting 20 and easting 21. The 5 is added after 10 because the church is approximately five-tenths of the distance between northing 10 and northing 11.

Try to find the exact six-figure grid reference for your local church, your house, or a nearby farm or lake.

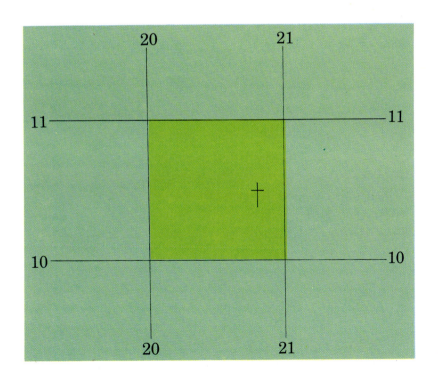

4. Atlasses

The round earth

The earth is so large that unless you actually look at it from space, you cannot get a very good idea of its shape. Not many centuries ago many people believed that the world was flat, and that you could fall off the edge! If you stand on the top of a hill and look at the horizon, it is quite easy to see how they got this idea.

Now we know that the earth is more or less round in shape, like a huge ball. You can get an idea of how gentle the curvature of the earth is by watching a ship going out to sea. First the hull of the ship disappears from view, then the deck and lastly the mast or funnel.

Covering the globe with a map

Maps are plans of countries or states on a round earth drawn on flat pieces of paper and this is where the problems begin. Try to cover a ball with a single piece of newspaper without leaving any gaps or pieces of paper overlapping. You may cut away the pieces of paper that would have overlapped. What shape are you left with?

Now try cutting and removing the peel of an orange so that the peel is left in one piece. Only three of these shapes will work. Which three are they?

Shapes and areas

When cartographers try to produce maps of very large countries such as Canada, the U.S.A. or the U.S.S.R., the curvature of the earth presents them with real problems. Curved shapes cannot easily be drawn on to flat surfaces.

So cartographers can either keep the correct shapes and area for the countries and cut up the map, like the one below:

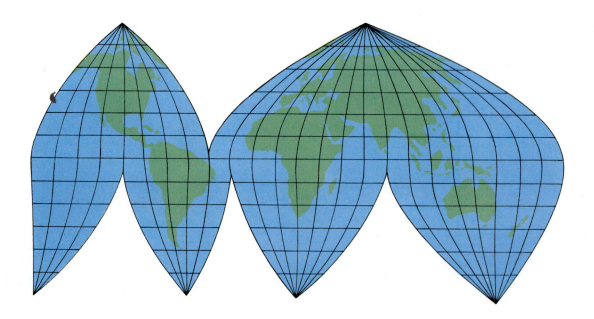

Or they can distort the shape and area to produce a map like this one:

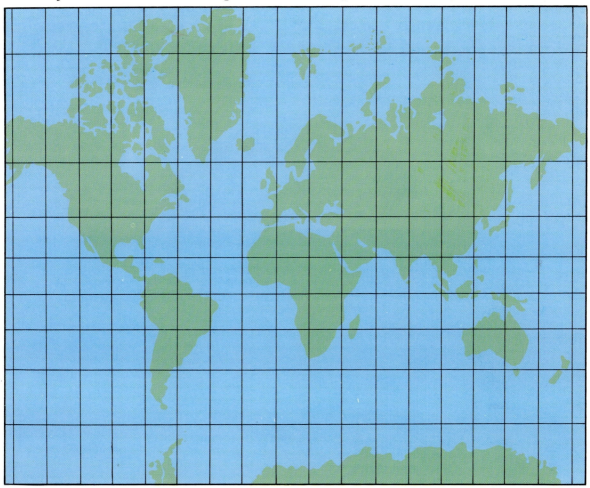

The different ways of drawing maps of the world are called projections. The projection on the opposite page is called a Sinusoidal projection. The projection on this page is called a Mercator projection. What happens to the northern coastlines of Canada, Greenland and the U.S.S.R. on the Mercator-projected map?

Look at your atlas and see how many different projections there are.

Latitude and longitude

Fixed base points and directions are needed to make world maps in exactly the same way as they were needed to draw your park map. Cartographers usually use the North and South Poles as their base points. The North and South Poles are the points about which the earth turns.

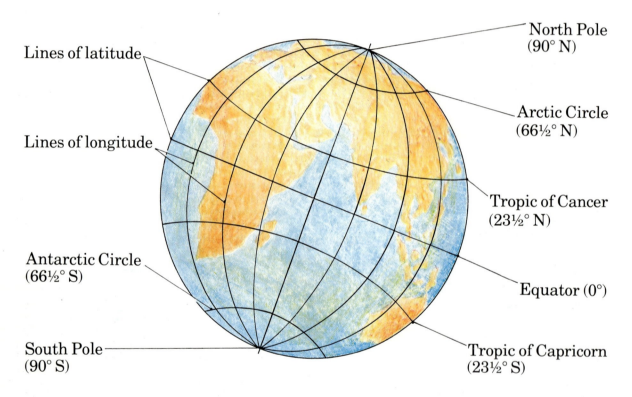

Cartographers draw half-circles from pole to pole. These are called lines of longitude. In the same way that compass bearings are divided into 360 parts, called degrees (see page 8) so there are 360 degrees of longitude.

The first line of longitude, 0°, is the Greenwich meridian. It passes through the Greenwich Observatory, near London. From this primary meridian, lines of longitude are drawn in each direction to 180°.

The line which joins up the mid-points of all the lines of longitude is called the Equator. The lines drawn parallel to the Equator are called lines of latitude. There are 180 degrees of latitude from 0°, which is the Equator, to 90° north (the North Pole) and 90° south (the South Pole). These, and the other important points of latitude, are shown on the globe opposite.

The exact position of any point on the surface of the earth can be fixed using longitude and latitude. For greater accuracy, each degree is divided into sixty minutes, which is usually written like this – 60'. For really accurate work, each minute is divided into sixty seconds (60'').

Work out the exact position in latitude and longitude for each of the islands shown below.

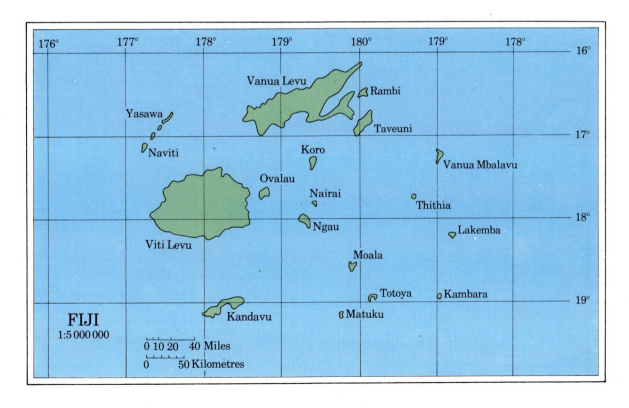

25

The 'norths'

There are three different northerly directions.

The position of the North Pole is called 'true north'.

A compass does not point exactly to true north. It points to a magnetic pole which is near the North Pole but not exactly at the North Pole. This pole is called 'magnetic north'.

On a grid for large-scale maps the eastings are all drawn parallel to one another. In fact they cannot really all point north because of the curvature of the earth (see pages 20-2). So the north on these maps is called 'grid north'.

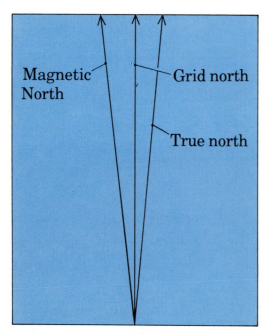

Look for the different north direction indicators on your local large-scale map.

5. Using maps

Maps on walks

The best map for use on walks is one drawn to a 1:25 000 or similar scale. Use the map to find the exact location of your house.

Now study the area within a 5-7-km (3-4-mile) radius of your home. Using the key, look for any places of interest – an old church, or archaeological site, for example. Now plan a route which will take you to the places of interest, using the footpaths marked on the map. Plan short routes to begin with. Use the contour lines to work out where the steepest hills will be. If you think they will be too steep, try to find an alternative route.

As you go along, mark your route in pencil on the map.

REMEMBER
Never walk long distances alone; always go with a friend.
Always tell an adult what you are doing, where you are going and when you expect to arrive home.
Never walk across unknown country in the dark unless you are with an adult.
Always take a compass with you.
If you get lost, use your map and compass to get you back to familiar country immediately.
Keep to recognized footpaths whenever possible.

Maps on cycle rides

For short cycle rides the best map is the 1:25 000 scale but if you are thinking of longer rides, then a 1:50 000 or even a 1:100 000 scale map will be best.

As with your walks, you should always go with a friend and you should plan your route carefully. Since you will be travelling greater distances, you will have to be even more careful in avoiding too many steep hills.

Plan a route that takes you along the quieter minor roads and unclassified roads. These often run through interesting villages and hamlets where you can stop to explore more of the countryside.

To get the maximum enjoyment from your ride in maximum safety, it is a good idea to section the route, and divide navigation between you and your friend.

Work out the grid references for each section and then take it in turns to navigate. Do not take over your section unless you are sure that you have both reached the agreed reference point.

Note the advice on page 27; always check that your bicycle is roadworthy, and make sure you know how to mend a puncture and how to make a call from a public telephone box.

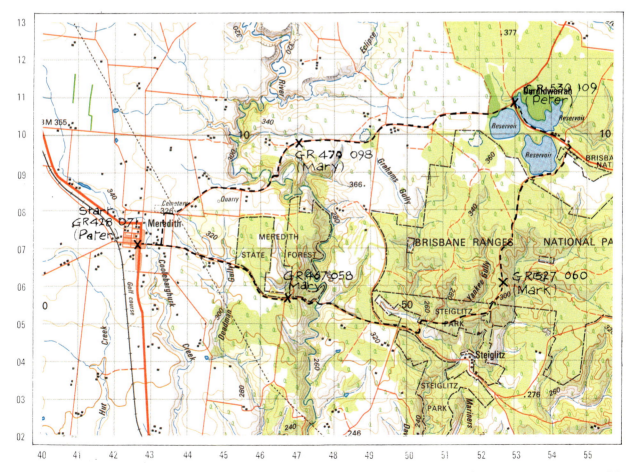

Maps on car journeys

On holidays, or on days when it is too cold for walking or cycling, you can improve your map-reading and navigation by taking your family or older friends on a mystery tour by car.

Again you will need to plan the route carefully using a 1:50 000 map (or its equivalent) or a 1:100 000 map. Plan the route using as few major roads as possible. Include villages and hamlets and places that you think might be interesting. Do not tell anyone else where you are going, but act as navigator for the driver.

Navigating

Mark the route that you intend to take on your map. Divide the route into short sections. Follow the route carefully as you go along. Remember that the driver does not know where he or she is going, so give your instructions in good time. Try to anticipate hazards like sharp bends or steep hills and warn the driver. Keep your instructions simple and limit them to the one or two miles immediately ahead.

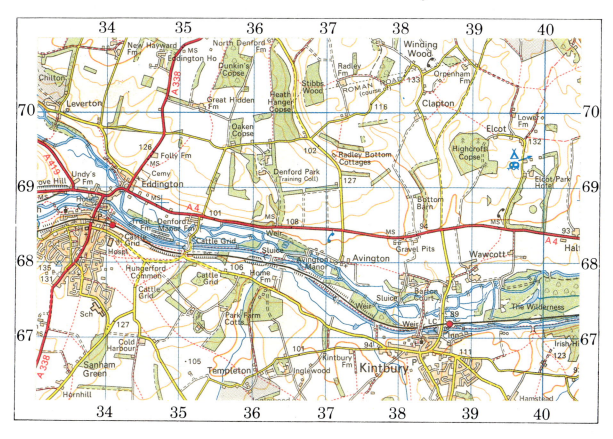

Using the above map, how would you navigate your driver from SU 356 695 to SU 351 681 to park the car near the railway crossing at SU 387 672?

31

Index

Atlasses 20-26

Bearings 8-9, 10

Compasses 8, 10
Contour lines 16-17

Eastings 18,19

Family maps 6

Grid north 26
Grid references 18-19

Keys 12

Latitude 25
Longitude 24, 25

Magnetic north 26
Maps
  definition of 4
  family maps 6
  home maps 7
  large-scale maps 14
  maps on car
    journeys 30-1
  maps on cycle rides
    28-9
  maps on walks 27
  park maps 10
  regional survey maps
    13
  small-scale maps
    14-15

Map-making 6-13
Mercator projection 23

North 26
Northings 18,19

Ordnance Survey 13

Projections 22-3

Scale 5, 14-15
Sinusoidal projection
  22, 23
Symbols 12

True north 26

Glossary

Curvature The amount by which a line or surface curves.
Cartographer A person who draws maps.
Grid A network of lines
Large-scale map A map on which a large area of map covers a small area of country.
Scale The size of a map or drawing measured in proportion to the actual area.
Small-scale map A map on which a small area of map covers a large area of country.